Enzo Carli

The Cathedral of Siena
and the Cathedral Museum

Edizioni Scala

Contents

© Copyright 1976 by
SCALA Istituto Fotografico Editoriale, Firenze
Photographs: SCALA
Design: Fried Rosenstock
Translation: Christine Smith
Produced by SCALA
Istituto Fotografico Editoriale, Firenze
Printed in Italy by La Zincografica Fiorentina, Firenze

The Cathedral

The Begininngs

The origins and first phases of the construction of the Cathedral of Siena are so obscure that even legend cannot illuminate them. Although it is one of the most prestigious, illustrious and artistically important cathedrals in Europe, the period and circumstances of its foundation are not known. We do not know what it originally looked like, and the chronology of its oldest sections is extremely uncertain, all of which raises innumerable questions still far from being solved.

According to tradition, the first Cathedral of Siena, dedicated to Saint Boniface, was built on the top of a hill known as Castelvecchio, which had previously been a Roman settlement. Here also an old tower may be identified as the prison of Saint Ansano, evangelizer and protector of the

town. But by the ninth century this church, with its Bishop's Palace, had been transferred to the present location and given the name of Santa Maria.

Although in 1058 it was the scene of the Synod that deposed the antipope Benedict X and elected Nicholas II, its dimensions must have been very modest. Almost certainly its orientation was perpendicular to the present Cathedral (that is, with the façade towards the Via del Capitano), and it occupied the space, now a square, between the façade of the present Cathedral and that of the Spedale. The legend that this space was once the site of a temple dedicated to Minerva, is completely groundless. An act of 1188 and a bull of Celestine III of 1193 demonstrate that at this time the orientation of the church had already

Nocturnal view of the city of Siena.

changed, and the façade was now opposite the Spedale.

Since 1196 there is evidence that a special deputation of citizens — the Opera di Santa Maria — was in charge of the construction which, however, was largely financed by the Commune, who provided the necessary materials and paid ten Masters who had sworn a special oath. In 1258 the direction of the Opera di Santa Maria was given to the monks of the Abbey of San Galgano, known to be expert administrators. They retained this position until 1314, accounting for their actions to the " Consiglio della Campana " (the Council of the Bell) or the Commune. However, it is extremely improbable that the Cathedral was founded by the famous Cistercian Abbey, since the Abbey was only begun around 1220, when the interior of the Cathedral was already in use, even if it was not entirely completed. Also improbable is the fifteenth-century belief that the Cathedral was consecrated on November 18, 1179, by Pope Alexander III of the Sienese family Bandinelli Paparoni whose standard, even now, is hung from the ceiling of the presbitery every year on that date and for the following week. However, that the ceremony of consecration was held, with various bishops in attendance, on November 18 of an unspecified year is proved by an ancient and unquestionable source: the *Ordo Officiorum Ecclesiae senensis*, a precious codex now in the City Library of Siena. The book, compiled in 1215 by Canon Oderico, confirms that masses were said daily in the church, and gives the location and dedication of its altars.

Since 1226, entries in the " Biccherna " registers — the registers of the financial office of the Commune of Siena — record payments for the transport of black and white marble which must have been used for the facing of the Cathedral and the Belltower (the latter finished by 1264). In 1259-'60 it was decided to construct vaults in the choir and transept of the Cathedral. Finally, in 1264, Rosso Padellaio (probably the same artist who, in 1227, had executed the bronze basin for the fountain in Perugia and a large bronze lintel for a side door of the Cathedral of Orvieto) was paid for the " apple ", a copper sphere on top of the dome. At this time attention was also given to the interior furnishing of the Cathedral. In 1259 Master Manuello di Ranieri and his son Parri were paid to carve some wooden choir-stalls, but these were replaced in the 1360's and have disappeared. Consequently, the earliest remaining work and the most precious of the many masterpieces that have enriched the Cathedral is the Pulpit, executed between 1265 and 1268 by Nicola Pisano with the help of his son Giovanni, of Arnolfo di Cambio, Lapo, and others. But, even before this date, members of Nicola's circle, if not Nicola himself, had worked in the Cathedral sculpting the grandiose figured capitals in the nave of the church. Later, around 1271, other followers of Nicola — Lapo, Donato and Goro — probably carved the main altar and the marble panels of the choir-screen.

In the last decades of the thirteenth century it was decided to replace the original façade of simple masonry with a new and sumptuous structure. The work was entrusted to Giovanni Pisano, the son of Nicola, who was Master of the Works between around 1284 and 1296. The lower level, where three broad splayed portals are surmounted by triangular gables, was probably built on his design. But Giovanni never saw the completion of what might have been his masterpiece: he departed suddenly from Siena, perhaps because of disagreements about the work. The construction of the façade continued for ten or fifteen years, then came to a halt, and, when it was resumed in the second half of the fourteenth century, it was with a new project. In 1287, while Giovanni was carving the admirable statues of prophets and philosophers intended to bring the façade to life, the Commune decided to provide the large round window of the choir with stained glass. This window was executed during the following year after designs by Duccio. In 1308 the famous Maestà — the altarpiece for the main altar — was commissioned from Duccio as

Aerial view of the Cathedral of Siena and Piazza del Campo.

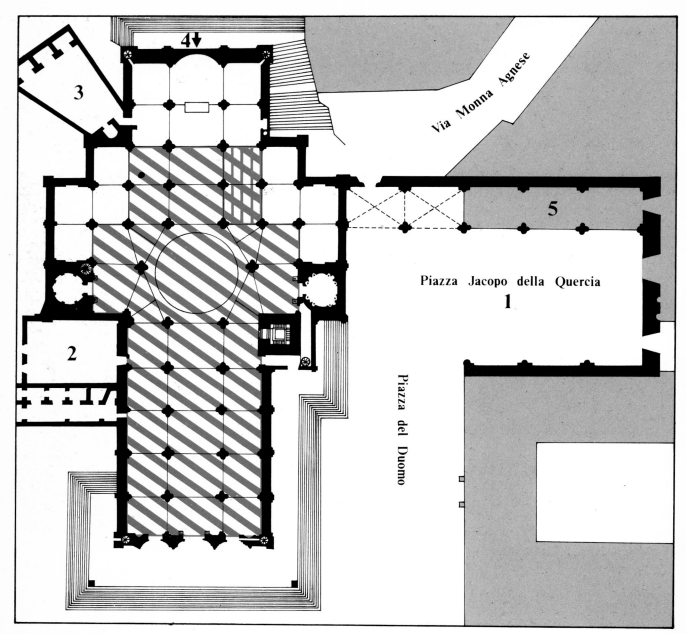

1 New Cathedral
2 Piccolomini Library
3 Sacristy
4 Baptistery
5 Cathedral Museum

Original plan
Remains of the Crypt

The Cathedral and the Belltower.

a replacement for the previous thirteenth-century one. Duccio delivered the work in 1311.

Until then the construction of the Cathedral, and the decoration of interior and exterior, had reflected a certain organic unity of purpose. The plan of the church was in the shape of a Latin cross with a slightly projecting transept, a dome, and a choir two bays long. The nave and the two side aisles are separated by rows of semi-circular arches, resting on compound piers. The length of the nave was then five bays, as it is at present. The structure also included a belltower with six levels of windows, the windows increa-singly wide with each successive level (as in Lombard style). The church stood, as it does today, on a wide platform raised above the level of the square. Today there are eleven steps, though originally there may have been twelve, symbolizing the twelve Apostles. Since the Bishop's Palace (destroyed in 1658) adjoined the right side of the church and the Chapter House adjoined the left, the lower parts of the side walls of the Cathedral were not visible. The dome, instead, was certainly visible although the lower part of the drum (decorated with a row of small arches on double columns) was partially obscured when the nave was raised in the fourteenth century. The choir was two or three steps above floor level and underneath it was a crypt, which is now more than two thirds underground. Recently the remaining portions of this crypt have been opened to the public and one can see the remains of important frescoes painted in the second half of the thirteenth century.

During the second decade of the fourteenth century the Sienese became more and more convinced that their Cathedral was too small. And, as we know from a contemporary chronicle, around 1317 the choir was extended above the steep slope called Vallepiatta. Beneath the new choir construction, space was allotted for a new Baptistery, in substitution for the old one situated near the Bishop's Palace (where today the Via del Capitano begins).

Although in 1332 a commission including Lorenzo Maitani (author of the façade of the Cathedral of Orvieto), opposed the project, work continued. The project was entrusted to Camaino di Crescentino (father of the famous sculptor Tino), and he completed the vaulted ceilings of the new Baptistery in 1325. Work on the walls of the new Cathedral choir had already begun above these vaults, when the Sienese conceived a bold new plan.

The Belltower and the dome of the Cathedral.

The façade with its three portals.

On August 23, 1339 the " Gran Consiglio della Campana " of the Commune decided on a further enlargement of the Cathedral consisting of a three-aisled longitudinal structure placed perpendicular to the south-eastern side of the existing church. This new structure was intended to serve as the transept of a new Cathedral, the apse of which was to have been beyond the dome to the west. Two precious documents in the Cathedral Museum show us two different plans for the project. Both agree in showing a nave of six bays, but they differ in the design of the transept and the apse. One retains the Latin cross plan, with a polygonal apse as wide as the central nave, while in the other plan the apse has become a huge semicircle — as wide as the transept — with radial chapels.

The foundation stone was laid on February 2, 1335, by Donusdeo Malavolti of Siena and Galgano Pagliaresi, Bishop of Massa. The director of the project was Lando di Pietro, a Sienese goldsmith, sculptor, and engineer, who had been recalled to Siena from Naples, where he had been working for Robert of Anjou. His annual salary of two hundred lire was paid in equal parts by the Commune and the governing body of the Cathedral. But he did not remain Master of the project long enough for us to be able to attribute to him, with any degree of certainty, either the credit for the grandiose scheme or the responsibility for its unfortunate end.

Several months before Lando died in August 1340, Giovanni d'Agostino had taken his place as director of the project. Under the direction of this artist, best known as a sculptor, work on the New Cathedral proceeded rapidly, not only in terms of the structure, but also of the marble facing and sculptural decoration. When work on the project came to a halt during the plague of 1348, the basic errors in construction were already evident: the foundations were too shallow and the building material of poor quality. The defects were more than serious, they were irreparable. Consequently in 1350 the new director, Domenico d'Agostino, proposed to abandon the entire scheme for the New Cathedral and simply to complete the extension of the old choir over the Baptistery. Many of the most reputable architects of the time supported the wisdom of this conclusion. For example, Benci di Cione, then working on the Cathedral of Florence, in a written report, strongly emphasized the danger of continuing work on the New Cathedral. Accordingly, the project was abandoned in 1355 and two years later the governing body of Siena ordered the demolition of the unsound sections. The interior columns on the left were to be saved for use in the construction of a new Baptistery and of a Camposanto (monumental cemetery) similar to that at Pisa; but, in the end, they too were demolished. A part of the exterior walls of the abandoned New Cathedral were left standing, and the right aisle was expanded to contain the offices of the governing body of the Cathedral. The façade wall, of such dizzying height that it was called the " facciatone " (great façade), remains in its original state of reddish masonry overlooking the whole town.

These imposing fragments of architecture, while not sufficient to permit a complete reconstruction of what the New Cathedral was to have looked like, nonetheless provide a good indication of the taste of the time, and suggest the extraordinary novelty and importance of the original scheme. In fact, the New Cathedral was the greatest, and perhaps the only opportunity in architecture, in which the Sienese were able to demonstrate their own stylistic preferences. A uniquely Sienese sense of form and mode of expression, deriving from a clearly-defined culture, had already been positively asserted in painting. The New Cathedral had offered a possibility to express the character of Sienese culture also in architecture. The feeling for line, typical of Sienese sensibility, was in fact the central stylistic element in the New Cathedral. This linearity is here pushed to its maximum possibility of expression, in fact to the point of endangering the stability of the structure. Yet

The ' facciatone ' (great façade) of the New Cathedral.

it does not explore those effects of vaguely defined and almost unbelievable sense of space which characterize Northern Gothic architecture. Nor does it, as in that style, convey the excitement of linear forms infinitely repeated and fantastically multiplied. In the New Cathedral, the linearity of the grandiose and yet subtle colonnettes neatly delimits the well-proportioned wall surfaces and the expanding spatial volumes: and although the majority of the arches are round rather than pointed (the latter being used only for windows) the effect remains Gothic.

The volumes and spaces are transformed into areas of color and their relation with the elements which define them is the same as that between the color patches and their enclosing contours which can be seen in a painting by Simone Martini, for example, or by Ambrogio Lorenzetti.

The area that was to be occupied by the main nave of the New Cathedral is so large that it is now a square. Once called after the Manetti brothers, it was renamed in 1938 in honor of Jacopo della Quercia. Standing in this square, one can examine the structure of the projected façade. Most striking is the immense window — perhaps more accurately described as a two-story loggia — which here substitutes the more traditional rose-window design. The wall is not just a plain masonry surface, but is enlivened by touches of color and design such as the window, the black marble stripes on the wall, and the delicate supports of the gallery. In particular one notes a band of multi-colored inlaid

11

The three doors of the
present façade,
built on designs
by Giovanni Pisano.

The middle door
of the façade.

This door of the New Cathedral was to have been a secondary entrance, directly into the right nave.

The marble sculptural group in the lunette above the door is attributed to Giovanni d'Agostino.

marble which, stretched across the entire length of the structure at the height of the side aisles, may be compared with the gold borders which adorn the robes of the Madonna and Saints in Sienese painting. Since the façade window is only slightly splayed, it retains that strong sense of depth which gives it the appearance of a loggia or a triumphal arch. Also to be noted is the use of classical decoration in the window as in other parts of the structure; for example, the capital, ornamented with cupids, in the right aisle. But this should not be considered a Gothic structure tempered by a classical sense of balance: in fact, classical form does nothing to moderate the almost fantastic and irrational character of this wholly Gothic creation. On the contrary, the light, the fame, the poetry of the ancient world must have inspired the architect (just as less than a century later they inspired the Sienese sculptor, Jacopo della Quercia), suggesting forms and ideas which he freely transformed and expressed within the architectural language of his own time. For this reason, the New Cathedral is not simply a masterpiece of Gothic architecture but, more precisely, a masterpiece of *Sienese Gothic* architecture, as

the Gothic style found here in Siena constitutes a unique mode of expression also to be recognized, of course, in Sienese painting.

Fortunately for us, the facing and the decoration of the New Cathedral were executed contemporaneously with the structure. Had they waited for the completion of the structure before turning to its decoration, as was the usual procedure, we could not admire today what is certainly the most elegant portal in all of Sienese art. This door was to have been the entrance into the right aisle of the new building, near the transept. Today it stands where the steep " Piaggia della Morte " (Slope of Death) joins the flight of steps leading to the Baptistery, as the visual point of transition between the stairs and the square. The slender proportions of the portal, its delicate shapes and the sharp brittleness of its pinnacles decorated with small statues suggests a huge piece of goldsmith's work mounted on the marble wall. In the lunette, created by the superimposition of a pointed arch on a flat arch, is a beautiful sculpted group of the *Enthroned Redeemer* adored by two genuflecting angels, a work attributed on rather flimsy evidence to Giovanni d'Agostino. To him

14

are also ascribed the statues of saints in the tabernacles and gables. Two small doors which give onto the loggia of the great façade possess delicate lunettes in bas-relief which may be attributed to Giovanni with greater certainty. One represents the *Madonna and Child*, and the other *Christ Blessing*. The location of these reliefs in a part of the building not accessible to public view demonstrates a desire of the Sienese to decorate the New Cathedral even in its less visible sections.

This little door is topped by a delicate lunette in bas-relief, sculpted by Giovanni d'Agostino.

Since the attempt to create the New Cathedral had failed, the Sienese resigned themselves to completing the extension of the choir of the already existing church. The transept was extended by one bay in each arm and enlarged to a width of three aisles. Between 1356 and 1359 Domenico d'Agostino constructed piers above the ceiling of the Baptistery which were to support the weight of the choir extending over it. The marble facing of the exterior of the Baptistery was begun following a design (now in the Cathedral Museum), often incorrectly attributed to the painter Jacopo di Mino del Pelicciaio, and probably to be dated in the second or third decade of the fourteenth century. The work, however, was left unfinished on the upper part of the façade. Beginning in 1376 work on the Cathedral façade was resumed under the direction of Giovanni di Cecco. The original project by Giovanni Pisano had only been carried out on the lowest level — that of the doors — when work came to a halt around 1330-'40. Now a new design was conceived, born of tastes and ideas quite different from those of Giovanni Pisano. In the intervening period the façade of the Cathedral of Orvieto had been designed and built by Lorenzo Maitani, and the new project for the Sienese façade shows its influence in the three large gables, the buttresses, the pinnacles and the large round window placed inside a square. At this time, (around 1370), in order to re-adjust the proportions of the now enlarged church, the height of the nave was raised above that of the small external arcade of the dome. The large quantity of materials, documented as having been acquired in the years following 1369, probably was used in this reconstruction. Once the nave had been raised, it became possible to build the façade up to its present height, certainly much higher than had been foreseen in the first project. But in some ways, the second façade project is but imperfectly connected with the earlier one. In fact, in order to avoid that the central zone of the upper part (the square with the round window) should seem too narrow, it was designed in such a way that it does not correspond to the division of the lower part. One can see that the pinnacles which flank the central zone of the upper part do not visually continue the columns and pinnacles flanking the central portal, but are, instead, suspended over the arches of the side portals. In addition, since the width of the striped wall areas at the extreme right and left of the lower zone determined the size of the polygonal towers added above, the towers seem far too squat. Remedies were sought for these serious structural defects. For example, the weight of the towers was reduced by opening windows in them. The stylistic impression of the façade is one of a constant and lively play of light and shadow, and of rich ornament, particularly in the small sculptural details. But above all the façade is characterized by its superb display of monumental sculpture. The statues (now heavily restored) representing *Prophets*, *Philosophers* and *Apostles*, were carved by Giovanni Pisano and his assistants. The half-length figures of *Patriarchs* in the niches around the round window, and the statues on the uppermost pinnacles of the façade are the work of other artists.

The lower zone of the present façade faithfully follows the conception of Giovanni Pisano, despite restorations of the jambs and cornices. The portal design is evidence of a sculptor's sensibility, especially in the deeply splayed doors and in the subtle contrast between the semicircular arch of the central portal and the slightly pointed arches of the side portals. The two columns on either side of the main portal are also by Giovanni Pisano and his workshop (these will soon be replaced by plaster models, now on view in the Chapter House). The columns are decorated with acanthus scrolls, biblical scenes and allegorical figures. The badly-weathered lintel with *Scenes from the Life of the Virgin* is original and unanimously attributed to Tino di Camaino.

Marble tondo by Donatello above the
'Porta del Perdono'.

It must be one of his earliest works, dating from the first decade of the fourteenth century.

Between 1458 and 1459 Donatello prepared wax models for the bronze central door, but these were never cast and the present door, representing the *Glorification of the Virgin*, was made by Enrico Manfrini in 1558. At least until the late fifteenth century the lunette of this portal contained a fourteenth-century marble group of the *Madonna and Child* with worshiping angels. In the seventeenth century this was replaced by a large bronze symbol of the name of Christ. In the same century, marble busts of the three Sienese saints, *Giovanni Colombini*, *Ambrogio Sansedoni* and *Andrea Gallerani*, were sculpted by Tommaso Redi in replacement for mosaics in the gables. We know that the lost mosaic of the central gable represented the *Lamb of God*. Since the nineteenth century, almost all of the

façade sculpture has been replaced by copies, which in most cases faithfully reproduce the originals housed in the Cathedral Museum. The three large mosaics of the gables which crown the façade were made in Venice in 1878. The central one, representing the *Coronation of the Virgin*, was designed by Luigi Mussini and those at the sides, with the *Presentation of Mary in the Temple* and the *Nativity*, are the work of Alessandro Franchi.

The left side of the church offers little of major importance, except for a fourteenth-century inscription marking the grave of Giovanni Pisano. This inscription, formerly on the façade of the Bishop's Palace (not its original site), was transferred in 1921 to its present position on the corner pillar of the Cathedral.

Along the right wall of the building the beautiful windows with pointed arches are decorated with

The 'Cript of the Statues'.

graceful fourteenth-century statues, which suggests that they must have been visible above the roof of the old Bishop's Palace which was built against that wall. In fact, the lower part of the wall was faced with marble only after the demolition of the Bishop's Palace. At the same time, the so-called " Porta del Perdono " was built in the Belltower, and in 1677 Donatello's lovely tondo of the *Madonna and Child* was placed in its lunette. The work was probably brought here from the fifteenth-century façade of the Cappella del Voto (Chapel of the Votive Offering). The bronze doors of the Porta del Perdono represent " four acts of Sienese devotion to the Virgin ". They were commissioned by Count Guido Chigi Saracini in gratitude for the fact that Siena was not destroyed during the Second World War, and were executed by the Sienese Vico Consorti in 1946.

Standing in the square to the right of the Cathedral, one can admire the Belltower with its narrow stripes and the dome, completed in 1264. Before the nave was raised, the small exterior arcade around the drum must have been completely visible. The dome was originally topped by a simple copper sphere, but in 1385 Barna di Turino replaced this with a small dome called " la mete minore ", also topped by a gilded copper sphere and a cross. The present elegant lantern was built in 1664 and the exterior of the dome was covered in lead-covered bricks after the fire in October 1890.

The large statues of the twelve apostles placed on the roof of the central nave and the right aisle create a rather strange effect. This is certainly not the location which they were intended for. The statues, by anonymous followers of Giovanni Pisano, were carved in the first decades of the fourteenth century and stood against the pillars inside the Cathedral until 1681. In that year, Giuseppe Mazzuoli replaced them with new statues which were removed around 1870 and subsequently acquired by the Brompton Oratory in London, where they may be seen today. The statues on the roof of the nave and aisles are, like those of the façade, copies of the originals. These are now kept in a room half way down the magnificent flight of steps (built in 1451 by Giovanni Sabatelli) to the right of the Cathedral, which joins Piazza Jacopo della Quercia with Piazza San Giovanni (that, is, the level of the Cathedral with the level of the Baptistery). This

The 'Cript of the Frescoes'.

room, rather inexactly called the "Crypt of the Statues", is open to the public and a visit to it is recommended. Besides these statues, some of which are of great quality, one can see the external wall of the Cathedral, at the point where the choir and the right transept meet, as it looked before the choir was extended. From this room one passes to another, placed under the first two bays of the right aisle, and which is all that remains of the crypt. Its walls are covered with frescoes (recently restored) representing the *Passion*, the *Madonna* and *Saints* which are extremely important in the history of Sienese painting. They were painted around 1270-'80 by an anonymous follower of Guido da Siena and are the earliest examples of Sienese wall painting which remain today.

What is most immediately striking and fascinating in the interior of the Cathedral is the vibrant pictorial effect of the black and white marble stripes which cover the walls, and the solemn succession of the powerful columns which support the arches of the nave. This interior is probably the most intense expression of that love of color which also characterizes other Tuscan Romanesque buildings from the Cathedral of Pisa to San Giovanni Fuorcivitas in Pistoia. In Siena these stripes have an added significance since the " balzana ", or civic coat-of-arms, is divided horizontally into two bands, one black and one white. Marvelous scenographic effects are produced by the dim lighting in the nave and by the perspective views of the hexagonal dome, of the transept, and of the deep space of the choir. In fact, Richard Wagner asked a painter-friend

*The interior
of the Cathedral.*

*The interior
of the Cathedral,
towards the entrance.*

Detail of the interior of the Cathedral.

The crossing seen from above.

of his to send sketches of this interior to serve as a model for the temple of the Holy Grail in *Parsifal*.

Above the triumphal arch which leads into the transept, one can still see a part of the small arcade which, before the nave was raised, surrounded the drum of the dome on the outside. (At least, this is the present interpretation of this peculiar feature). Another, even more difficult problem is posed by the capitals of the front part of the nave carved with allegorical busts and animals. Stylistically these capitals may be attributed to followers of Nicola Pisano — per-

haps even to the young Arnolfo di Cambio — and consequently cannot have been sculpted before the second half of the thirteenth century. However, we know that the Cathedral was in use, and therefore structurally complete, by 1215. Either the Cathedral was reconstructed in the period between 1215 and 1260, or the capitals were put into place as rough blocks before 1215 and only later carved. The possibility of Nicola Pisano's participation in this hypothetical reconstruction may find confirmation in the strongly projecting cornice which encircles the nave. This horizontal cornice visually breaks the vertical

The inside of the dome.

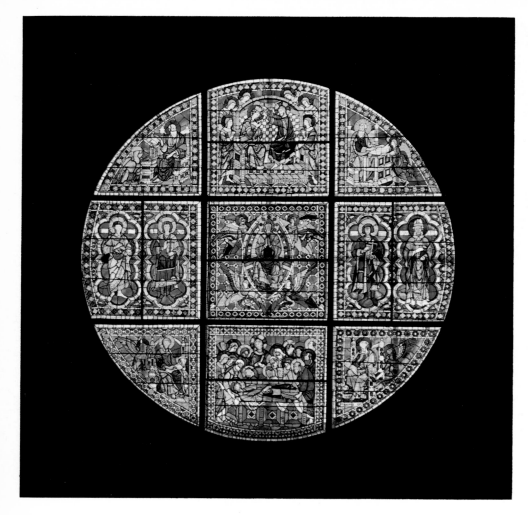

*The circular
stained-glass window
of the choir.*

impulse of the half-columns which rise from the floor to the ceiling. The motif is typical of Romanesque architecture in Puglia, where Nicola was born and it was probably Nicola himself who introduced it to Tuscany. The motif later became popular and was used in the Cathedral of Orvieto, in that of Florence and in Santa Croce also in Florence. In Siena the horizontal line is weighted down by the later addition of 171 plaster busts of popes, beginning with St. Peter and ending with Lucius III. The busts are mediocre works of the fifteenth and sixteenth centuries.

At the end of the perspective of colonnades, the circular window of the choir shines with its clear kaleidoscopic colors. The window, which used to be called " the wheel " or " the eye of glass ", was made in 1288 and in 1365 it was moved from the old choir wall to the new one. The subjects represented are the *Evangelists*, the four *Patron Saints* of Siena, the *Entombment*, the *Assumption* and the *Coronation of the Virgin*. Duccio di Buoninsegna designed the cartoons for this, one of the earliest examples of Italian stained glass. In some of the designs, for example the *Coronation*, he introduced themes which he was to develop twenty years later in the *Maestà*. The circular window of the façade is also very beautiful: here the *Last Supper* is presented in a grandiose composition. The work was designed by Perin del Vaga and executed in 1549 by Pastorino de' Pastorini, a student of the famous master Guillaume de Marcillat. The pedestals of the columns on either side of the portal below contain bas-reliefs of the *Life of the Virgin* by Urbano da

24

The circular window of the façade.

Cortona (1483) which were brought from the old Cappella del Voto, while the two richly carved columns are the work of Giovanni di Stefano (1483) and came from the altar of the church of Santi Quattro Coronati in Rome.

General view of the marble floor towards the entrance.

The marble mosaic floor of the Cathedral has always aroused wonder and admiration in all who see it and, for its vast extent alone, it may be considered unique. Covering the entire floor area of the Cathedral, it is divided into fifty-six panels of various sizes and it contains elegantly framed representations of *Sibyls*, *Biblical Stories*, *Virtues* and *Allegories*. Some of these images have been restored or even re-made, but the majority still retain their original characteristics. It is interesting to observe how, in the course of two centuries, the technique evolved from a simple " graffito " (that is, drilling holes and lines in the marble and then filling these in with bitumen or mineral pitch) in which the panels resemble enormous woodcuts, to an intarsia of multi-colored marbles and finally to a technique in which a mosaic of grey and white marble is enlivened by the addition of colored pieces. The most surprising and delicate effects of light and shadow, comparable to the effects of painting, are obtained with this last technique. Vasari had credited Duccio di Buoninsegna with the earliest work on these marbles, but the first from 1369 and '70, long after his death. According to Sigismondo Tizio, a Sienese chronicler of the sixteenth century, the *Wheel of Fortune* (in the last bay of the nave before the transept) was laid in 1372.

The documents of 1369 and '70 do not indicate which portion of the floor was executed in those years, and unfortunately the assertion of Tizio cannot be verified on stylistic grounds since the *Wheel of Fortune* was heavily restored in 1864 by Maccari. Also uncertain is the date of 1373, rather vaguely mentioned in another old chronicle, for the panel in the second bay of the nave. This panel, also heavily restored in 1865, represents the *Sienese She-Wolf* surrounded by the emblems of twelve confederate cities. The earliest panels, which can be dated with any certainty, are those of the *Four Cardinal Virtues* and the figure of *Mercy* in the presbytery, on either side of the main altar and in front of the choir-stalls. A payment of March 1406 to Marchese d'Adamo and his

General plan of the floor of the Cathedral, preserved in the Cathedral Museum.

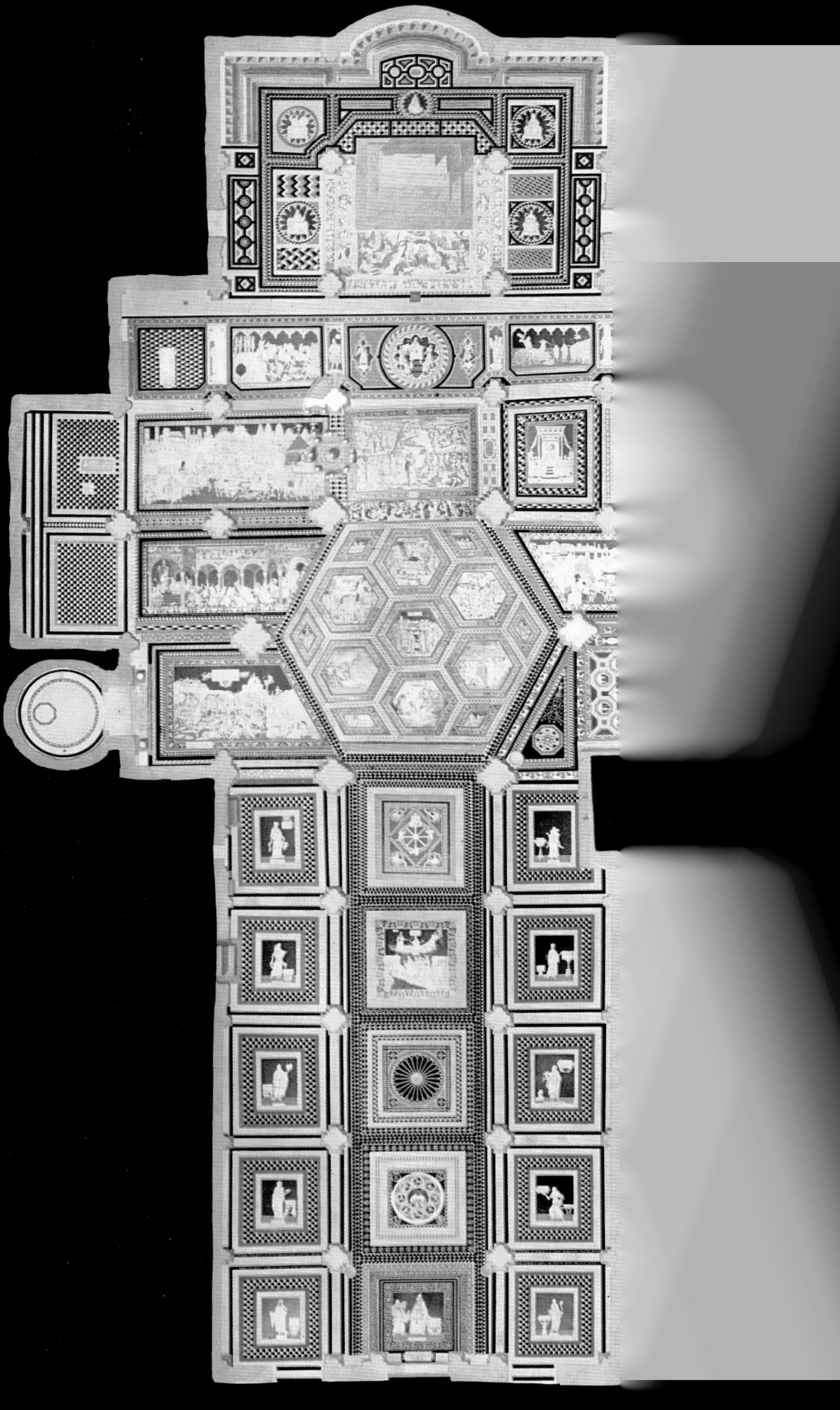

The History of Fortune or the Hill of Virtue, on designs by Pinturicchio.

" fellow stone-masters from Como " seems to refer to one of the Virtues (*Fortitude*). Unfortunately, these figures were also restored in the last century so that one cannot make stylistic judgments, but their iconography suggest that Marchese d'Adamo and his fellow-workers, until now considered the authors of the *Virtues*, were in fact simply the technical executors of cartoons provided by one or more Sienese painters.

The first well-known artist who worked on the mosaic floor, perhaps both as designer and as " spianatore " (marble-worker), was Domenico di Niccolò dei Cori, a famous sculptor who was Master of the Cathedral Works between 1413 and 1423. We know with certainty that he executed the panels of the story of King David; that is, *David the Psalmist* and *David and Goliath* in the second bay after the transept. These scenes are rather well preserved. The first, *David the Psalmist*, is of particular interest also for the study of the history of music since the four musicians around the king carry instruments typical of the period; while in the *David and Goliath* the physical act of throwing the stone is so concretely represented that one could almost suppose it to have been designed by Jacopo della Quercia. To Paolo di Martino, Domenico di Niccolò's successor as Master of the Works, are attributed two large scenes on either side of the stories of David. These, representing the *Victory of Joshua with the Hanging of the Five Amorite Kings* and the *Victory of Samson over the Philistines*, were completed between 1424 and 1426. We know very little about Paolo di Martino's other activity: only

Domenico di Niccolò:
David with his Sling.

Domenico di Niccolò: David the Psalmist.

that in 1414 he assisted in the decoration of the choir-stalls in the chapel of the Palazzo Pubblico, but his work was found unsatisfactory and the commission was given to Domenico di Niccolò. The well-known painter Domenico di Bartolo was paid in 1434 for the panel of *Emperor Sigismund Enthroned Surrounded by Four Counsellors and Two Pages.* Apart from the elegance of the composition, already Renaissance in character, the scene is significant proof of the popularity of the King of Luxembourg with the Sienese. This king, accompanied by his brilliant court, spent ten months in Siena while waiting to be crowned in Rome.

Next to the panel of Sigismund is the *Death of Absalom*, vigorously composed and among the most beautiful of the series. We know only that

it was begun in 1447, when Pietro di Tommaso del Minella was Master of the Cathedral Works. This architect-sculptor probably designed the panel, although the execution differs slightly from that of the tomb of Bishop Carlo Bartoli, a documented work by Pietro.

In 1473 work on the Cathedral floor was begun again. The panel representing *Stories from the Life of Judith and the Liberation of Bethulia* was probably executed by Antonio Federighi on designs by Urbano da Cortona or Matteo di Giovanni. The Master of the Works, Savino di Matteo Savini, was replaced in 1480 by Alberto Aringhieri who held this position for many years, and strongly supported the mosaic floor project. In fact it was under his supervision that the ten panels of the *Sibyls* (1481-'83), in the side aisles, were

*Pietro del Minella (?):
Death of Absalom.*

*Urbano da Cortona (?):
Stories from the Life of
Judith and the Liberation
of Bethulia.*

Neroccio di Bartolommeo: Hellespontian Sibyl.

Vito di Marco: Cumaean Sibyl.

designed and carried out. These Sibyls are the most charming representations of women in fifteenth-century Sienese art. Although extensive restorations have spoiled the original delicacy of their outlines, one can still admire the variety of their poses, the elegance of these graceful figures set against a red and black background and the imaginative design of their lecterns and richly flowing robes. Some of them were designed by major artists; for example the *Samian Sibyl* was designed by Matteo di Giovanni, the *Hellespontian* by Neroccio di Bartolommeo, and the *Albunian* by Benvenuto di Giovanni. These three are probably the most beautiful.

But those designed by Vito di Marco (or perhaps his shop) — the *Cumaean, Delphic, Persian,* and *Phrygian Sibyl* — arouse our curiosity about this obscure German master. Unfortunately, the *Erythrean Sibyl*, a signed work of Antonio Federighi,

has been so extensively reworked that we can no longer appreciate its style. The same is true for the *Libyan Sibyl*, designed by the painter Guidoccio Cozzarelli. But despite its restorations, the boldly designed figure of the *Cumaean Sibyl* is so similar to that of *Hermes Trismegistus* (a semi-mythical sage) in the first bay of the nave, that one recognizes the style of Giovanni di Stefano.

Some of the artists who designed the Sibyls also designed other parts of the mosaic floor. For example, the famous *Massacre of the Innocents* (1481) may be considered the work of Matteo di Giovanni, since we know that he is the author of three paintings on the same subject in the same style. Also, in 1484-'85 Benvenuto di Giovanni designed the *Expulsion of Herod*, remarkable for the variety of movements and poses in the crowd. The last scene commissioned by Aringhieri is in the fourth bay of the

Guidoccio Cozzarelli: Libyan Sibyl.

Vito di Marco: Delphic Sibyl.

nave — the *History of Fortune*, or *Hill of Virtue* — designed by Pinturicchio in 1504 and executed by Paolo Mannucci in 1506. In this allegorical representation, inspired by Humanist thought, Fortune helps some wise men reach a mountainous little island after a storm at sea. On the summit of this island Knowledge offers the palm of victory to Socrates, while Crates empties a chest of jewels into the sea. The panel, although restored in 1859 under the direction of Luigi Mussini, is still striking for the balance of its composition, its elegant design, and the lovely color contrasts of black sky, red mountains, and grey-green sea.

The artist who made the most important contribution to the floor was Domenico Beccafumi, the greatest Sienese artist of the sixteenth century. In fact, between 1518 and 1524 he designed four of

the seven hexagons and two of the six rhombuses in the transept with *Stories from the Life of Elijah.* In 1525, he executed the enormous frieze (more than 8 meters long) representing *Moses Striking Water from the Rock*, and in 1531, the stories of *Moses on Mount Sinai*. Finally, in 1547, he did the scene of the *Sacrifice of Isaac* in front of the main altar.

In the thirty years during which Beccafumi worked on the Cathedral floor his style evolved from a Raphaelesque Classicism (as in Raphael's Loggias in the Vatican) to the new Mannerist style, seen in the impressive composition crowded with figures in motion. This evolution of style is paralleled in the development of the technique of the marble inlay, increasingly characterized by vibrant contrasts of light and dark, and a pictorial freedom which, in its use of patches of color, becomes

Giovanni di Stefano:
Hermes Trismegistus.

Matteo di Giovanni: Massacre of the Innocents.

very modern, almost Impressionistic. In the face of this excitingly modern expression, the panels completed, and those partially restored, by Alessandro Franchi in the last quarter of the nineteenth century seem pale indeed, and coldly academic.

Domenico Beccafumi: Sacrifice of Isaac.

Detail of the Sacrifice of Isaac.

34

The Cathedral and Baptistery of Siena constitute an important museum for the study of Italian sculpture during its most glorious centuries. Some of the greatest Italian sculptors, who worked in the four centuries between the Romanesque and Baroque periods, have left masterpieces in these buildings. The greatest of these is probably Nicola Pisano's pulpit carved between the end of 1265 and November 1268. Like his pulpit for the Baptistery in Pisa (completed in 1260), the pulpit in the Cathedral of Siena is concerned with the Christian doctrine of Salvation and the final destiny of humanity. The octagonal pulpit is supported by nine columns ; the staircase was built in 1543 by Bartolomeo Neroni, called " il Riccio " The overall structure of the pulpit and its supporting

Nicola Pisano:
Pulpit.

Nicola Pisano: Visitation and Nativity.

Nicola Pisano: Adoration of the Magi.

Nicola Pisano: Presentation and Flight into Egypt.

Nicola Pisano: Massacre of the Innocents.

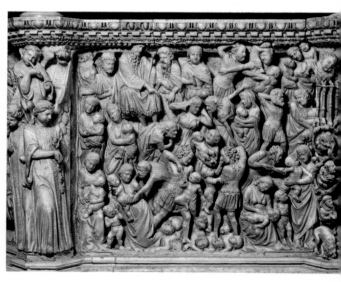

columns is divided into three levels, each with a precise symbolic meaning. In the lowest part, (slightly raised off the ground in the sixteenth century, when the pulpit was moved from the entrance of the choir to its present position) the columns are supported by lions and lionesses, except for the central column, which is supported by the *Seven Liberal Arts* and *Philosophy*. This was the first time that the *Liberal Arts* were included in the decoration of a church interior and they probably represent the intellectual means through

which man may perceive God. Each of the eight corners of the intermediate level (the top of the columns and the base of the pulpit itself), bears a small statue of a Christian *Virtue* and in the spandrels over the threefoiled arches are *Evangelists* and *Prophets* who, respectively, reveal and announce the Salvation of man. The theme of Salvation is fully explored in the seven panels of the top level with scenes from the life of Christ and the *Last Judgment*. Between the reliefs are statues, among them a lovely *Madonna and Child*.

Nicola Pisano: detail from the Crucifixion.

Nicola Pisano: Last Judgment (panel representing the Blessed).

Nicola Pisano: Crucifixion.

Nicola Pisano: Last Judgment (panel representing the Damned).

In the Siena pulpit, Nicola further developed the Romanesque style with strong Classical overtones which had characterized his Pisa pulpit. Probably his discovery of Northern Gothic art accounts for the new plasticity and freedom of the forms and for the way in which light caresses the delicately modelled surfaces. While the Pisa pulpit is a solemn celebration of the events of Christ's life, here Nicola penetrates into the emotions of his figures, who seem passionately aware of the unfolding drama. Note, for example, the anxiety in the *Visitation* and the warm affection of the *Nativity* in the first panel; the picturesque description of the Magi and their journey in the *Adoration* in the second panel; the candour of the *Presentation in the Temple* and the moving sadness of the *Flight into Egypt*, in the third panel; the dramatic conflict between the desperate mothers and the soldiers in the *Massacre of the Innocents*, which foreshadows the martyrdom of the equally innocent Christ, in the fourth panel. The last panel of the stories from the life of Christ is the *Cruci-*

Tino di Camaino: Tomb of Cardinal Riccardo Petroni.

fixion — the most beautiful scene in the cycle. Here, the fragile body of the suffering Christ and the swooning form of the Virgin are particularly touching because they are contrasted with the group of persecutors. In the two reliefs of the *Last Judgment* (on either side of the statue of *Christ the Judge*) the faces of the Blessed and of the Damned are such realistic portraits that they

Jacopo della Quercia: Madonna.

Andrea Bregno: Piccolomini Altar.

Paolo di Giovanni Fei: Madonna and Child.

transform the biblical event into a scene of immediate and modern reality.

Among Nicola's assistants in the project were the young Giovanni Pisano and Arnolfo di Cambio, whose presence may be detected in the work. For example, Arnolfo seems to have worked on the earlier scenes (from the *Visitation* to the *Presentation*) while Giovanni helped carve the *Massacre of the Innocents* and the figure of *Christ the Mystic* between the fourth and fifth panels. The complete homogeneity of the style, despite the participation of various artists, indicates the constant supervision of Nicola. The entire work is so

original that it has been described as representing the destiny of Italian sculpture.

The work of Tino di Camaino, the foremost Sienese sculptor of the fourteenth century (also active in Pisa, Florence and Naples), is represented in the Cathedral by the tomb of Cardinal Riccardo Petroni, a famous jurist who died in Genoa in 1314. The monument, built between 1317 and 1318, is the finest and earliest example of fourteenth-century funerary architecture and was used as a model throughout that century. It is composed of a sarcophagus decorated with statues and reliefs and supported by four caryatids. Above the sarcophagus, curtains are drawn apart by angels,

Donatello:
Tombstone of
Giovanni Pecci,
Bishop of Grosseto.

Lorenzo di Pietro:
Ciborium.

revealing the effigy of the dead man with two guardian-angels. A tabernacle with the Madonna and Saint Peter and Saint Paul crowns the monument. The broad and powerful forms are characterized by compact volumes and soft contours.

Jacopo della Quercia, Lorenzo Ghiberti and Donatello — the three greatest fifteenth-century sculptors — worked together on the font in the Baptistery. Jacopo, the only one of the three who was Sienese, had already worked in the Cathedral at the very beginning of his career. The marble *Madonna* at the top of the Piccolomini altar, dated 1397-1400, may well be his first work. And, after his work in the Baptistery, he again took up work in the Cathedral, where he supervised the decoration of one of the chapels until his death in 1438. His remarkable carved relief in the Cathedral Museum was intended for that chapel.

Donatello's contribution to the Cathedral includes the *Madonna* above the " Porta del Perdono " (discussed above), the bronze tombstone of Gio-

Francesco di Giorgio Martini:
Angel with candelabra.

Domenico Beccafumi:
Angel with candelabra placed against a presbytery pier.

vanni Pecci, Bishop of Grosseto, in the Chapel of Sant'Ansano, beneath the tomb of Cardinal Petroni and a bronze statue of *Saint John the Baptist* (1457) in the chapel of the same name. The forceful drama of this figure, one of the masterpieces of Donatello's late style, is similar both in style and in spiritual content to the more famous statue of *Mary Magdalene* in Florence.

Sienese sculptors of the second half of the fifteenth century found the Cathedral an ideal place in

41

Neroccio di Bartolommeo:
Wall tomb of Bishop Tommaso Piccolomini del Testa.

which to practice their art. The splendid bronze *ciborium* over the main altar was made in 1472 by Lorenzo di Pietro (" il Vecchietta "). Originally commissioned for the church of Santa Maria della Scala, it was taken to the Cathedral in 1506 because of its great artistic worth. One admires the exquisite grace of the *musician angels*, the sweetness of the *Virtues* seated in niches, and the lightness of the angels and of the *Resurrected Christ* at the summit, all perfectly united within an overall composition of rare clarity. On either side of the ciborium, on the projections of the altar designed in 1506 by Baldassarre Peruzzi, are two pairs of bronze angels holding candelabra. The taller pair were sculpted by Giovanni di Stefano, son of the famous Sienese painter Sassetta, in 1488. This sculptor also made the marble statue of *Saint Ansano* in the Chapel of Saint John. The lower pair, elegantly executed, were made at the same time by Francesco di Giorgio Martini, who was not only a painter and a sculptor, but also one of the most celebrated architects of the Renaissance. Eight magnificent angels holding candelabra are placed against the presbytery piers, as a visual introduction to the richly furnished altar. Domenico Beccafumi sculpted these in the last years of his life (1548-'50). They demonstrate his ability to translate into bronze the same light-filled vivacity and freshness found in his paintings. But, to return to the sculpture of the fifteenth century, we must consider the work of Antonio Federighi: the two highly ornate holy-water fonts at the entrance of the church, and a basin for the blessing of holy-water on Holy Saturday. The basin was later used as a baptismal font and transferred

Antonio Federighi:
Holy-Water Font.

to the Chapel of Saint John. These three works display that particular trend of studied classicism which characterized Sienese sculpture in the last quarter of the fifteenth century. The same style is evident in the decorated pedestals of the columns at the entrance to the Chapel of Saint John. In fact, one of these was commonly thought to be an ancient Roman altar, here re-used as a column base. The chapel itself was built in 1481 to house an important relic — the right arm of Saint John the Baptist. Pope Pius II, who had received the precious relic from Thomas Palaeologus (the exiled despot of Morea), donated it to the Cathedral of Siena. In this chapel we may admire the marble statue of *Saint Catherine of Alexandria*, which was carved in 1487 by Neroccio di Bartolomeo Landi, one of the most delicate and spiritual of Sienese painters. Neroccio had proved his ability as a sculptor four years earlier in the wall tomb of Bishop Tommaso Piccolomini del Testa. This wall

43

Michelangelo: Saint Paul.

Michelangelo: Saint Peter.

tomb may be seen above the small door which leads to the Belltower.

The glory of sixteenth-century Italian sculpture is represented by the " divine " (as Vasari called him) Michelangelo. This man of genius also gave his contribution to the Cathedral of Siena. Michelangelo was asked to carve fifteen statues for an altar which had been commissioned by Cardinal Francesco Piccolomini and executed in 1481 by the Lombard Andrea Bregno. But Michelangelo only carved four of these between 1501 and 1504, when he was attracted to Florence by the more prestigious commission of the *David*. The first is the proud and beautiful *Saint Paul*, probably a self-portrait; then the gentle and pensive *Saint Peter*, the melancholy *Saint Pius* and *Saint Gregory*, in which the help of an assistant is most evident. Although these statues are securely documented and, except for the last, entirely by his hand, they are among the least well-known works of the young Michelangelo.

The Cappella del Voto (Chapel of the Votive Offering).

The last great sculptural enterprise at Siena Cathedral was made possible by an illustrious Sienese pope, Alexander VII, of the Chigi family. In 1659 he commissioned the German architect Schor to build the Cappella del Voto (Chapel of the Votive Offering) following designs by Bernini. The new chapel, replacing the fifteenth-century chapel by Urbano da Cortona, was intended as a setting for the much-venerated " Madonna del Voto ". This painting was once part of a larger composition done in the second half of the thirteenth century by an anonymous follower of Guido da Siena. The original painting commemorated the vow made by the Sienese on the eve of the famous battle of

Bernini: Saint Jerome.

Bernini: Mary Magdalene.

Montaperti (September 4, 1260) in which they dedicated the town of Siena to the Virgin.

The chapel is circular in plan with a gilded dome supported by eight columns brought here from the Lateran Palace in Rome. Stylistically, the chapel is a masterpiece of the purest Roman Baroque. At the entrance is an elegant bronze gate by Giovanni Artusi (called " il Piscina "). Within the chapel are four niches containing marble statues of saints: a statue of *Saint Bernardino* by Antonio Raggi, and a *Saint Catherine of Siena* by Ercole Ferrato, who also designed the gilt-bronze angels against a lapis lazuli background which surround the image of the Madonna. Bernini is the author of the passionate, almost delirious, *Saint Jerome* and of the *Mary Magdalene* which, because of its ardent sensuality and the dramatic way in which the nude form emerges from the flowing robes, was once thought to be a pagan statue of Anromeda.

The decoration of the chapel is further enriched by four bas-reliefs with the *Life of the Virgin* by the Roman artist Pietro Bracci and by two large paintings by Carlo Maratta — the *Visitation* and the *Flight into Egypt.* This last was in such bad condition by 1793 that it was re-made as a mosaic.

Mattia Preti:
Saint Bernardino
Preaching.

The Cathedral was once rich in famous altarpieces painted by the major Sienese artists of the fourteenth and fifteenth centuries; by Duccio di Buoninsegna and Simone Martini, by the two Lorenzetti brothers, by Sassetta and Matteo di Giovanni. All of these were removed when the altars were restored at the end of the sixteenth century. Some of these precious works — Duccio's *Maestà* for one — are now kept in the Cathedral Museum, while others have found their way to the Uffizi (among these, the famous *Annunciation* by Simone Martini, the *Presentation in the Temple* by Ambrogio Lorenzetti and, most recently, the *Ma-donna of the Snow* by Sassetta), and still others have been entirely lost. Of all of this original decoration only the small and gentle *Madonna and Child* attributed to the fourteenth-century artist Giovanni di Paolo Fei still remains in the church (now on the Piccolomini altar). Of the large altarpieces which now fill the Cathedral, only a few are of any artistic interest. One may note an *Adoration of the Shepherds* by Alessandro Casolani (1594), the *Saint Ansano Baptizing the Sienese* by Francesco Vanni, (1596) and *Saint Bernardino Preaching* (1650) with the violent " chiaroscuro " contrasts typical of Mattia Preti, a follower of Caravaggio. Behind the main altar is a very large

47

Alessandro Casolani: Adoration of the Shepherds.

Assumption of the Virgin painted in 1594 by Bartolomeo Cesi.

The documents record that many well-known masters created frescoes for the walls and the ceilings. All of the ceiling decoration has been replaced by a blue background strewn with gold stars. Another unfortunate loss is the fresco cycle of Old Testament scenes done between 1404 and 1406 for the presbytery by Taddeo di Bartolo and Spinello Aretino.

The oldest frescoes now remaining are in the three chapels of the new sacristy commissioned in 1408-'09 by the Administrator of the Cathedral Caterino di Corsino. These frescoes, discovered under layers of plaster in 1906, were executed between 1410 and 1412 by Nicola di Naldo da Norcia, Be-

nedetto di Bindo, and Gualtieri di Giovanni da Pisa. The stories of the four Patron Saints of Siena, painted in the same sacristy by Domenico di Bartolo between 1435 and 1440, are now lost. The "trompe l'oeil" coffering of the dome was done in the late fifteenth century, and in 1481 Guidoccio Cozzarelli and Benvenuto di Giovanni painted forty-two Patriarchs and Prophets in the colonnade which ornaments the drum. The eight large stucco statues beneath the dome were made by Ventura di Giuliano Turapilli and Bastiano di Francesco in 1490. These stucco works, originally polychromed and then gilded in 1704, represent the *Patron Saints of Siena, Saint Bernardino*, and *Saint Catherine.* Here one should note that, leaning against the two first pillars beneath the cupola, are two long standards, covered in leather, which probably accompanied the Sienese " carroccio " (the ox-drawn chariot, used in battle as the rallying point) into the battle of Montaperti. The same is said of the large wooden *Crucifix* over the first altar in the left arm of the transept, which dates from the late fourteenth century; but there is no evidence of this.

The large walls of the choir are covered with frescoes. Beccafumi began work here in 1544 by representing various *Saints* and *Paradise* on the walls and conch of the apse. (Unfortunately, these were partially painted over in 1912.) The project was resumed and brought to completion between 1608 and 1611 by Ventura Salimbeni, a Sienes working in the elegant style of late-Mannerism. On the side walls are his *Fall of Manna*, with a luminous landscape background; *Esther Pleading for the Hebrews*, a well composed scene in a solemn architectural setting; and two lively rows of *Saints*, most of them Sienese.

*The Chapel
of Saint John the Baptist.*

Detail of a decorated pedestal of one of the columns at the entrance to the Chapel of Saint John.

The most beautiful and famous frescoes in the Cathedral are not by a Sienese artist, but by the Umbrian Bernardino di Betto, " il Pinturicchio ". Born in Perugia around 1454-'55, he spent the last part of his life decorating the Chapel of Saint John and the Piccolomini Library in the Cathedral of Siena, where he died in 1513.

Pinturicchio worked in this chapel between 1504 and 1505, in the interval between his first and second contract for the Library. The Master of the Cathedral Works, Alberto Aringhieri, commissioned him to paint two portraits and six *Stories from the Life of John the Baptist*. Of these, two scenes — the *Baptism of Christ* and the *Beheading of John the Baptist* — were repainted in the seventeenth century by Francesco Rustici (" il Rustichino ") and a third — *John the Baptist in Prison* — was entirely re-done in 1868 by Cesare Maccari. The scenes now left by Pinturicchio are the *Nativity of John the Baptist* (retouched by Rustichino), *John the Baptist in the Desert, John the Baptist Preaching*, and the two portraits. These represent *Aringhieri with the Cloak of the Order of the Knights of Malta*, and a *Kneeling Knight in Armour*, who may in fact be the young Aringhieri entering the Order.

The two portraits are more worthy of admiration than the slightly affected *Stories of John the Bap-*

50

Donatello:
Saint John the Baptist.

Pinturicchio:
John the Baptist
in the Desert.

Pinturicchio:
John the Baptist
Preaching.

Pinturicchio: Nativity of John the Baptist.

Pinturicchio: Kneeling Knight in Armour.

Pinturicchio: Aringhieri with the Cloak of the Order
of the Knights of Malta.

tist, particularly that of the young knight. He seems a fairy-tale creature, his face transfigured in prayer, against a luminous landscape painted with an almost Flemish love of detail. The other portrait is more sharply drawn with the figure clearly set against a background representing the

gulf and fortress of Rhodes. These are an exquisite prelude to the frescoes in the Library, Pinturicchio's masterpiece.

The left-hand part of the choir.

While discussing the Cathedral we should also mention the choir, which contains the most impressive wood carving in Siena. The choir, begun in 1363 and finished in 1397, originally consisted of more than ninety choir-stalls arranged in a double row and crowned by an ornate canopy. Large tabernacles stood on either side of its entrances while others adorned the piers near the dome, and a large quantity of statues of saints, gaily polychromed and gilded, were to be seen everywhere. A great many artists worked on the project, the most important of whom were Francesco del Tonghio and his son Jacopo, Mariano d'Angelo Romanelli, and Barna di Turino. This splendid complex was dismantled, and the remaining thirty-six stalls are now against the terminal walls of the side aisles. Over each stall is the bust of a saint in a small pointed arch and the backs of the stalls have carved panels added by Fra' Giovanni da Verona in 1503 (originally made for the

Fra' Giovanni da Verona: carved panel of a choir-stall.

Wooden choir-stalls.

monastery of San Benedetto fuori Porta Tufi). In the apse itself are fifteen superb choir-stalls, carved with exquisite decorative exuberance between 1567 and 1570. These were executed by Teseo Bartolini da Pienza and Benedetto di Giovanni da Montepulciano on designs by Bartolomeo Neroni (" il Riccio "), who also designed the massive lectern behind the high altar.

The Piccolomini Library

The construction of the Piccolomini Library was begun in 1492 on the site of the old Chapter House. Commissioned by Cardinal Francesco Piccolomini Todeschini, then Archbishop of Siena and later to become Pope Pius III, the library was intended to house the extensive collection of books belonging to his uncle Pope Pius II and to honor the memory of this great Humanist. Approaching the library from the left aisle of the Cathedral, one notices a finely carved marble wall monument with two arched openings. This was carved in 1497 by Lorenzo di Mariano, " il Marrina ". In the left arch is the door to the Library, while the right contains an altar placed there in 1805. Above the altar is a tondo relief of *Saint John the Evangelist* attributed to Giovanni di Ste-

Marble façade of the Piccolomini Library.

The interior of the Piccolomini Library.

fano and below the altar table is a polychromed wooden group of the *Pietà*, sculpted by Alberto di Betto da Assisi in 1421 for the Chapel of the Crucifix. It seems that this artist was a protégé of Jacopo della Quercia, whose influence is evident in the powerful figures who convey an intense pathos. Above the cornice of the marble structure there is a large fresco representing the *Papal Coro-*

nation of Pius III, executed by Pinturicchio in 1504. The work was commissioned by the heirs of this pope who had held the papacy for only eighteen days when he died on October 18, 1503. The fresco has a crowded and labored composition, and is valuable only for some good portraiture. The identification of Pandolfo Petrucci, tyrant of Siena, with the figure behind the dog is surely

The ceiling of the Piccolomini Library.

The Three Graces.

false, since a deep animosity existed between the Petrucci and the Piccolomini. The upper part, where the head of the pope has been raised in stucco relief, was heavily restored in 1586 and again in 1812.

Passing through the graceful bronze gate, built in 1497 by Antonio Ormanni, the visual impact is unforgettable: having left behind the dimly lit and austere church, one enters a room full of light and enlivened by colors of an incredible freshness and variety. In the center of the room is the fa-mous marble group of the *Three Graces*, a good Roman copy of an original Greek painting. The work was purchased in Rome by Cardinal France-sco expressly for the Library. The ceramic floor is decorated with half-moons on a blue back-ground — the emblem of the Piccolomini family. The walls and ceiling are entirely covered with frescoes whose colors — never retouched or clean-ed — are wonderfully preserved. The ceiling, which Pinturicchio and his assistants executed between 1502 and 1503, is divided into panels

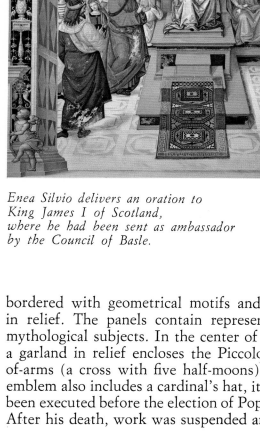

*Enea Silvio delivers an oration to
King James I of Scotland,
where he had been sent as ambassador
by the Council of Basle.*

*Enea Silvio Piccolomini (the future Pius II)
departs for Basle as secretary to
Cardinal Domenico Capranica.
Capranica is going to lodge a complaint
at the Council of Basle against Eugene IV
who had not wanted to consecrate him cardinal.
The group embarked at Piombino and were driven
to the coast of Africa by a storm,
visible in the background.*

bordered with geometrical motifs and gilt studs
in relief. The panels contain representations of
mythological subjects. In the center of the ceiling
a garland in relief encloses the Piccolomini coat-
of-arms (a cross with five half-moons). Since the
emblem also includes a cardinal's hat, it must have
been executed before the election of Pope Pius III.
After his death, work was suspended and then re-

Enea Silvio is crowned poet by Emperor Frederick III, to whom he was sent by the anti-pope Felix V, elected in Basle.

Enea Silvio gives his allegiance to the legitimate pope, Eugene IV, who then (scene in the background) consecrates him bishop.

sumed from 1505 to 1507. In that year Pinturicchio finished the ten scenes on the walls, illustrating the glorious events of the life of Enea Silvio Piccolomini, Pope Pius II. The story begins in the corner next to the large window on the right wall and each scene contains an explanatory inscription in Latin.

These ten stories are admirable above all for the fantasy with which Pinturicchio could infuse a theme so arid and prosaic as the public life of a diplomat. Enea Silvio, first a high prelate and then pope, moved in courtly circles among officials whose every gesture was determined by rigid protocol. In this case the painter's tendency to daydream — in so many of his works a negative factor — enabled him to enliven the tedium of those

Enea Silvio is ordained cardinal by Pope Calixtus III.

Enea Silvio, bishop of Siena,
who had arranged the marriage between Frederick III
and Eleanor of Aragon, presides over the meeting
of the betrothed couple at the Camollia gate in Siena.
This is the most famous scene of the cycle because
of the quantity of portraits and the rich costumes
which reproduce the traditional iconography
of the Marriage of the Virgin in a wordly
and fashionable context.

genuflections, of that foot-kissing, of those speeches and those solemn assemblies of cardinals. He introduced elegant pages and graceful youths into the narrative and set his scenes against idyllic landscape backgrounds filled with light. Through the gleaming marble arches of the ceremonial halls one sees blue-green bays crowded with ships and

The Papal Coronation of Pius II (September 3, 1458).
The Lateran sexton kneels before the pope
in the gestatorial chair and sets fire to a wad of flax,
to symbolize the transitory nature of wordly glory.

Pius II gathers the Christian princes at Mantua
to organize the crusade against the Turks.

sunny squares with airy porticoes and fabulous palaces. The eye is enchanted by clear, cold skies where fat ducks and rapacious hawks fly, by grassy hills upon which slender Umbrian poplars and Tuscan cypresses grow, and where the mossy pastures of an imagined Scotland are reflected in the pale translucence of Lake Trasimene. And it is on the strength of these delightful details, rather than on the rigidity of the narrative scenes, devoid of drama and of human warmth, that Pinturicchio's cycle must be judged. In this, his masterpiece, the painter retained the freshness and the interest in nature typical of the Late-Gothic style within the context of a High Renaissance work.

The Canonization of Saint Catherine of Siena.

Pius II, already ill, arrives in Ancona
(where he died two months later, on August 15, 1464)
to hasten preparations for the crusade.
In the background, the Venetian fleet arrives.

Unfortunately, the Greek and Latin codices which
were the pride of Enea Silvio are now lost. These
books, once kept in cases and shelves carved by
Antonio Barili gave this library, created by a pope,
annexed to a Cathedral by a cardinal and watched

Liberale da Verona:
Aeolus.

Girolamo da Cremona:
Adoration of the Magi.

Liberale da Verona: the Wood-Cutters.

over by three pagan nudes, an exclusively secular and Humanist character. But one can still admire the splendid psalters illuminated by Liberale da Verona and Girolamo da Cremona for the sacristy of the Cathedral, and these surely represent all that was fine and rich in the art of fifteenth-century illumination. Liberale, who arrived in Siena in 1466 when he was only twenty, and Girolamo, who arrived in 1468, were engaged in the illumination of twenty-nine psalters and anthem-books begun by the Sienese Pellegrino di Mariano. After their departure (in 1478 and 1474 respectively), the work was carried on by other Sienese painters: Sano di Pietro, Guidoccio Cozzarelli and Benvenuto di Giovanni. The presence in Siena of these two Northern masters, particularly of Girolamo whose style was rooted in the Mantegna tradition of the Paduan school, had its effect on the direction of Sienese painting in the late fifteenth century. On the other hand, Sienese art had, in its turn, an influence on Liberale.

The Baptistery

The Baptistery occupies a large space beneath the last two bays of the extended choir of the Cathedral. Its interior, largely constructed under the direction of Camaino di Crescentino and finished about 1325, is rectangular in plan, divided into three aisles by two robust piers. The valuted ceilings are covered with frescoes representing *Articles of the Faith, Prophets* and *Sibyls*, painted by Lorenzo di Pietro (" il Vecchietta ") between 1447 and 1450. The cycle must originally have been of

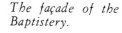

The façade of the Baptistery.

great artistic value and among the most important works produced in fifteenth-century Siena, but now it can only be appreciated for its iconography since it was repainted towards the end of the last century. Also by Vecchietta are two scenes from the life of Christ (the *Flagellation* and the *Way to Calvary*) on the walls of the apse. The frescoes in the conch of the apse — the *Agony in the Garden*, the *Crucifixion* and the *Lamentation* — were painted in 1477 by the Late-Gothic master Michele di Matteo da Bologna. The lunette at the end of the left aisle has a fresco of the *Miracles of Saint Anthony* by Benvenuto di Giovanni, perhaps designed by Vecchietta, dating from around 1460. The mediocre canvas on the altar of the *Baptism of Christ* was painted in the nineteenth century by Alessandro Franchi.

The greatest art treasure of the Baptistery is the

The interior of the Baptistery.

Lorenzo di Pietro:
Articles of the Faith.

The apse of the Baptistery.

font, the reliefs and statues of which constitute the most important anthology of Italian sculpture of the Early Renaissance. The frames and the tabernacles at the corners, on the other hand, are still Gothic in taste. These were begun in 1417 by Sano di Matteo, Nanni di Jacopo da Lucca, and Jacopo di Corso da Firenze on a design erroneously attributed to Jacopo della Quercia. The reliefs and gilt brass figures are the work of Lorenzo Ghiberti, Jacopo della Quercia, Donatello and some minor Sienese artists. They illustrate the *Life of John the Baptist* and begin (on the side facing the altar) with the *Annunciation to Zacharias* made in 1428-'29 by Jacopo della Quercia, who here shows himself aware of the style of the two great Florentines who also contributed to the font. The next panels are those of the *Birth of John the Baptist* and the *Baptist Preaching* by Giovanni di Turino (1427),

The baptismal font.

Jacopo della Quercia: Annunciation to Zacharias.

Lorenzo Ghiberti: Baptism of Christ.

and then follows the *Baptism of Christ* (1427) by Ghiberti of exquisite delicacy. Ghiberti and Giuliano di Ser Andrea together are the authors of the

following scene, the *Arrest of John the Baptist.* Finally *Herod's Banquet* is by Donatello (1427). The work is highly original not only for the in-

Lorenzo Ghiberti: Arrest of John the Baptist.

Donatello: Herod's Banquet.

Donatello: Faith.

Donatello: Hope.

tensity of its drama, but also for its exploration of perspective composition.

Two of the six corner statues are by Donatello (1429): the gentle figure of *Faith*, and *Hope*, fervent in prayer. The figures of *Justice*, *Charity* and *Providence* are by Giovanni di Turino, and *Fortune* (1431) is by Goro di Ser Neroccio. The heavy marble tabernacle in the center of the basin was probably not part of the original plan. It was designed between 1427 and 1429 by Jacopo della Quercia who also carved the five vigorous statues of prophets in the niches. Turini ornamented the door of the tabernacle with a delicate *Madonna and Child*. Between the gables of the tabernacle are six graceful bronze angels. Two are by Donatello (the one dancing and the one playing the trumpet), three by Turini and the sixth is anonymous. At the top is a marble statuette of John the Baptist by Jacopo della Quercia. Another statuette of John the Baptist, this one in polychromed wood, is by Jacopo's workshop and stands in a niche in the left wall.

The Cathedral Museum

General view of the Hall of the Statues in the Cathedral Museum.

The Cathedral Museum was created in 1870 by closing in three bays of the right aisle of the New Cathedral. This space had once served as a workshop for the Cathedral sculptors, and here Jacopo della Quercia carved the *Fonte Gaia* for the Piazza del Campo. The Museum, which contains works of art belonging to the Cathedral, is perhaps the richest and most important of its kind in Italy. Among the numerous paintings, sculptures in marble, wood, bronze and terracotta, goldsmith work, tapestries and embroideries, the Museum possesses two works of fundamental importance for the study of the history of art: the statues made by Giovanni Pisano for the Cathedral façade, and the *Maestà* by Duccio di Buoninsegna, originally on the main altar of the Cathedral.

*Jacopo della Quercia:
Cardinal Antonio Casini
presented to the Virgin
by Saint Anthony Abbot.*

The first floor consists of one large room which houses the marble statues. The room is divided in two by a lovely wrought-iron gate (fourteenth-century) brought here from the Spedale della Scala, and whose emblem we can still see — a cross at the top of a small ladder.

This gate is supported by four marble panels with heads and ornamental designs in bas-relief. These

*Giovanni Pisano:
She-Wolf with
the Twins.*

Giovanni Pisano: Sibyl.

Giovanni Pisano: Plato.

four, plus two others nearby, were once part of the choir-screen by Nicola Pisano. Another panel (in fragmentary state) representing a veiled female head — perhaps symbolizing the Church —

surrounded by the four Evangelists, was once part of the main altar. One of Nicola's assistants — probably Lapo — is the author of this fine piece. On the same wall is a sarcophagus, a Ro-

Giovanni Pisano: Detail of Mary sister of Moses.

man work in Hellenistic style, showing the deceased surrounded by Tritons and Nereids. Nicola Pisano used one of the Nereids as a model for one of the Blessed in the panel of his pulpit depicting the Last Judgment.

On the other side of the wrought-iron gate, in the center of the room, is a high-relief showing *Cardinal Antonio Casini presented to the Virgin by Saint Anthony Abbot.* The relief, from the Chapel of Saint Sebastian (destroyed in 1645) in the Cathedral, was commissioned by Cardinal Casini and sculpted by Jacopo della Quercia during the last days of his life: Jacopo died on October 20, 1438. The relief is a work of an extraordinary power and plasticity, expressed in the rich drapery folds and in the melancholy face of the Virgin. The floor and lower parts of the walls of the room are covered with worn fragments of the Cathedral mosaic floor. Particularly worthy of note are the fragments representing the *Ages of Man* by Antonio Federighi (1475).

Along the walls are the statues carved by Giovan-

Giovanni Pisano: Mary sister of Moses.

Giovanni Pisano: Habakkuk.

Giovanni Pisano: Moses.

ni Pisano between 1284 and 1296 for the façade of the Cathedral. These were removed to the Museum in the mid-nineteenth century, in order to protect them. Considered as a whole, the cycle has no precedent in Italian art. The grandiose

scale, the elevated conception and the technical excellence of these statues are proof of the new direction taken by Italian art at the moment when Northern Gothic sculpture had lost its impetus, sinking into a preoccupation over minute detail.

Giovanni Pisano: detail of Simeon.

Here, instead, one feels the energy of new and varied formal solutions and a totally new stylistic vision of monumental sculpture.

These statues are larger than life-size and they represent biblical figures, prophets, philosophers of classical antiquity, and the two prophets of Judaism and Paganism; Mary sister of Moses, and the Sibyl. All of these figures, according to Medieval religious thought, foretold the immaculate conception of Mary, to whom the Cathedral is dedicated, and the coming of Christ. But what most sets this work apart from the more famous sculptural cycles of the great Gothic cathedrals in France and Germany is the fervour with which each figure carries on a passionate, formal and spiritual dialogue with its companions, each one revealing at the same time its own unmistakable individuality. There is great variety between the prophetic

Giovanni Pisano: Bull.

Perhaps the most beautiful of them all is *Mary Sister of Moses*, whose body turns in a slow spiral beneath her flowing Gothic drapery. She leans anxiously forward, nostrils quivering and mouth half-opened, totally enraptured by the mysterious prophecies she hears.

One of statues of the *She-Wolf with the Twins* — the emblem of Siena — is also by Giovanni Pisano: the other version of this subject, rather weakly carved, is by Urbano da Cortona. A copy of the Pisano group is now on a column on the Cathedral steps. On the wall opposite the window there are five more works by Giovanni: three lions, one of them winged, a horse and a bull (this last is heavily restored). Higher up on the same wall are the *Patriarchs* and *Prophets*, who once surrounded the round window of the façade as did the *Madonna and Child*. Once attributed to Giovanni di Cecco, this was more probably executed by an unknown Sienese sculptor in the years 1320-'30. The statues of the *Apostles* may be attributed to followers of Giovanni, while the large altarpiece of the *Baptism of Christ*, once in the Baptistery, was painted in 1524 by Andrea and Raffaello Piccinelli (" i Brescianini "). These painters based their own lively style on that of Fra Bartolomeo and Andrea del Sarto.

majesty of *Isaiah*, whose classical features are filled with sweetness, and the vehement eloquence of *Plato*; the meek and wise *Solomon*, and the sharp and nervous spirituality of *Moses* are in evident contrast with the restless pathos of *Habakkuk* and the raging fury of *Simeon*, whose glaring eyes flash from beneath his wild mane of hair. The figures are firmly rooted to the ground, yet reaching out freely into space: they are as solid as columns and yet as light as Gothic pinnacles. The somewhat motionless forms of the classical *Sibyl*, of the *David* and of the *Daniel* are in contrast with the almost Baroque freedom of the *Aristotle* (whose head was re-carved in the sixteenth century) and of the *Balaam* or with the violent juxtaposition of planes and volumes in the *Haggai* and the already mentioned *Simeon*.

Duccio di Buoninsegna:
Madonna of Crevole.

Duccio's *Maestà* is the most famous and precious painting — or rather, group of paintings — of the Middle Ages in Europe. It was commissioned on October 9, 1308 by the Administrator of the Cathedral Works, Jacopo del fu Giliberto de' Marescotti, for the high altar. When Duccio completed it, after thirty-six months of work, on June 9, 1311, the entire population of Siena, led by the Clergy and the " Signoria " and accompanied by musicians, carried it in a solemn procession, from the painter's workshop, through the town, to the Cathedral. Three days of festivity followed, during which the Sienese showed not only their deep religious devotion and civic pride and their gratitude to their divine " Protectress ",

but also their admiration for the recently completed masterpiece. A chronicler of the time records the total cost of the work as 3,000 gold florins, a sum so exaggerated that we should probably consider it a mistake for 300. Even this amount is enormous and much greater than any other painter of the time had received.

Originally the large altarpiece, in addition to being painted on both sides, had a predella and pinnacles. In 1506 the painting was removed from the high altar and in 1771 the front and back were separated and exhibited in two different chapels in the Cathedral. Finally, in 1878, the work was transferred to the Museum, but in the meantime

Duccio di Buoninsegna: Maestà (front).

(top panels, starting
from the left)
Christ again before
Pilate and Christ
before Herod

The Flagellation and the
Crowning of Thorns

The Way to Calvary
and Pilate washing
his hands

The Crucifixion

The Entombment and the
Deposition from the Cross

The Holy Women at the
Tomb and the Descent
into Hell

The Appearance at
Emmaus and
'Noli Me Tangere'

(bottom panels, starting
from the left)
The Entry into
Jerusalem

The Washing of Feet
and the Last Supper

The Betrayal of Judas
and Christ's Farewell

The Kiss of Judas and
the Agony in the Garden

Christ before Anne and
Peter denies Christ

Christ Mocked and Christ
before Caiaphas

Christ accused by the
Pharisees and Christ
before Pilate

Duccio di Buoninsegna:
Maestà (back).

80

parts of it had been lost. Eight of the predella panels are no longer in Siena: three are in the National Gallery in London, two in the National Gallery of Washington, and one each in the Frick Collection in New York, the Thyssen Collection in Lugano, and the Fort Worth Museum in Texas. One panel has simply disappeared. Some of the upper panels, four or six belonging to the front and back of the central portion, and eight half-length figures of angels from the pinnacles are also lost (four others are in foreign collections). In addition, the entire carved wooden framework which must have been very elaborate and beautiful, has disappeared. What is now in the Museum are the front and back of the central portion, seven predella panels and twelve panels originally above the main scenes. The theoretical reconstruction of the entire work has been attempted many times,

Duccio: detail of two angels from the front of the Maestà.

Duccio: detail of the Madonna from the front of the Maestà.

but there is still no certainty as to how it originally looked.

The front of the central panel is formed by a single composition (2.12 meters high and 4.25 wide) of the enthroned Madonna and Child adored by almost life-size figures of saints and angels representing the heavenly court. At the left side of the throne are *Saint Catherine of Alexandria, Saint Paul, Saint John the Evangelist* and various angels; at the right are *Saint John the Baptist, Saint Peter, Saint Agnes* and ten angels. Kneeling in the foreground are the four Patron Saints of Siena:

Duccio:
detail of Saint Catherine
from the front
of the Maestà.

Duccio: panel of the predella with the Massacre of the Innocents.

Duccio: panel of the predella with the Flight into Egypt.

Ansano, *Savino*, *Crescenzio* and *Vittore*, and at the top are ten half-length figures of *Apostles*. On the platform of the throne is the inscription MATER SANCTA DEI — SIS SENIS REQUIEI — SIS DUCIO VITA — TE QUIA PINXIT ITA. (O Holy Mother of God — grant peace to Siena —

grant life to Duccio — since he has thus painted you). This inscription states the civic importance of the work in that the Madonna is invoked as a peace-giver for the city. But it also shows the artist's conviction that he has created a masterpiece and that, therefore, he may ask particular protec-

Duccio: *Entry into Jerusalem.*

Duccio: *Kiss of Judas.*

Duccio: *Washing of Feet.*

Duccio: *Agony in the Garden.*

tion from the Virgin. In this work Duccio integrated the Byzantine pictorial tradition, in which he was educated, with the Gothic spirit of the West, creating an entirely new style which was to be an example to all later Sienese painting. The rigorous, almost architectural composition underlines the super-human beauty of the figures, absorbed in the ecstasy of adoration and inner beatitude.

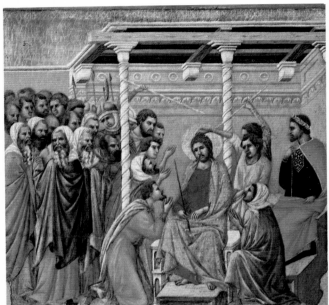

Duccio: Crowning of Thorns.

Duccio: Christ before Anne and Peter denies Christ.

Duccio: Way to Calvary.

The figure of the Virgin dominates the composition because of her size (larger than that of the other figures) and because of her spatial isolation effected by the throne whose sides are splayed like the jambs of a portal. Monumental and solemn, her imposing mass is softened by the Gothic rythms of her blue robe silhouetted against the

gold-embroidered cloth on the back of the throne. Her regal dignity is humanized by the loving inclination of her head and by her lowered glance, gentle and penetrating, as she receives the prayers of the faithful kneeling at her feet.

The panels of the predella and of the gables above the central part are arranged in two rows along

Duccio:
Crucifixion.

the wall of the same room, while on the adjoining wall are the panels from the back of the central portion. These recount, in fifty-three narrative scenes, the life of Christ and the last part of the life of the Virgin. The narrative begins on the front of the predella, divided into seven panels separated by six figures of Prophets. These contain stories from the childhood of Christ (the first two are missing). Christ's public life is recounted in nine scenes on the back of the predella, six of which are missing. On the back of the central portion are twenty-six panels of different sizes, illustrating the Passion from the *Entry into Jerusalem* to the *Appearance at Emmaus*. The narrative continues on the back of the gables (six panels) with the other appearances of Christ after the Resurrec-

Duccio:
Deposition
from the Cross.

Duccio: Holy Women at the Tomb.

88

Duccio: 'Noli Me Tangere'.

*Duccio: Panel of the gables
with the Doubting of Saint Thomas.*

tion and with the *Pentecost*. Finally, the last events of the Virgin's life are depicted in six panels on the front of the gables.

These scenes are unequaled in their clarity, technical excellence and sensitive coloring. Here the old iconographic schemes of the Byzantine tradition, which Duccio combines with a new Gothic taste and sensitivity, lose all their rigidity and seem brought back to life by the ability of the artist to capture the most subtle and intensely lyrical aspects of each event.

One of the loveliest scenes of the predella, the *Flight into Egypt*, has all the grace of a Hellenistic relief. The stories of the *Passion* on the back show a deep meditation on Christ and the events faithfully depict the Gospel narrative. High peaks of formal perfection and of evocative intensity are reached in the *Entry into Jerusalem*, where the raging of the crowd outside the city gates seems softened and almost kept at a distance by the little wall and the orchard in the foreground, the *Agony in the Garden*, the *Betrayal of Christ*, and the *Crucifixion*, which is much larger than the

other scenes, as was the Byzantine custom. Also of the highest quality are the *Deposition*, with the tender and pathetic expression of the Madonna, the *Holy Women at the Tomb* where the event seems suspended in a magical atmosphere emanating from the brilliant presence of the angel, and the *Noli Me Tangere*, with its barren rocky background. Among the scenes in the gables, perhaps the most striking are the *Annunciation of the Death of the Virgin*, a scene of classical composure; the *Virgin Taking Leave of the Apostles*, serene and solemn; and the *Funeral of the Virgin* outside the crenellated walls of Ephesus.

One may admire two other masterpieces of Sienese painting in the same room. The *Madonna of Crevole* (called after the Church of Santa Cecilia a Crevole, where it comes from) is unanimously considered the earliest extant work of Duccio and was painted around 1283, when he was still strongly tied to the Byzantine tradition. The *Birth of the Virgin* by Pietro Lorenzetti, signed and dated 1342, is this artist's last known work, and was originally on the altar of San Savino in the

Duccio: panel of the gables with the Annunciation of the Death of the Virgin.

Duccio: panel of the gables with the Virgin Taking Leave of the Apostles.

Cathedral. Here Pietro discards the traditional tri-partite division of the altarpiece and, by representing a continuous interior in the central and right panels, he has created an entirely new concept of pictorial space. In addition, he has interpreted the scene in terms of contemporary appearance (the costumes, the furnishing of the bedroom) without thereby diminishing the religious content. In the left panel a rapidly receding perspective construction, created by the succession of the arches and by the courtyard, provides the setting for Joachim, who bends forward to hear the news of the birth, brought to him by a child. There are three rooms behind that of the *Maestà.* In the room at the left are displayed accurate reconstructions (made in the nineteenth century) of the Cathedral mosaic floor and, in the glass cases, the earliest illuminated anthem-books and psalters of the Cathedral. Of these, four are from the thirteenth century and five from the fourteenth. Number 4 is particularly interesting, with its five miniatures painted in 1345 by Lippo Vanni, the major follower of Pietro Lorenzetti. In the two rooms at the right are more illuminated psalters, various documents relating to the artists who worked on the Cathedral, and a group of architectural drawings. Two of them show projects for the New Cathedral and one, a drawing for the Belltower in Florence, has recently been attributed to Giotto. Others are projects for the chapel of

Duccio: panel of the gables with the Funeral of the Virgin.

90

the main square of Siena and for the façade of the Baptistery (this can be dated around 1320-'30). The importance of these drawings is incalculable not only for the study of the history of these buildings, but also because they are among the oldest architectural drawings that we possess.

Pietro Lorenzetti: Birth of the Virgin.

On the third floor of the museum is the "Sala del Tesoro", the Hall of the Treasure, which contains a very rich collection of goldsmith work. The *Reliquary of the Head of Saint Galgano*, of gilded silver and filigree with opaque enamel, was made in the late thirteenth century. While the overall style may be described as Early Gothic, French, Byzantine, and German influence is also discernible as well as influence from the art of Nicola Pisano. Also of great value is the *Silver Urn for the Arm of John the Baptist*, executed in 1466 by the Sienese Francesco d'Antonio. The artist was strongly influenced by his teacher Giovanni di Turino and also by Ghiberti and Donatello. Hanging on the walls are large altar frontals of silk, embroidered in gold and silver, which depict the life of Christ and various saints. These were made in the early sixteenth century by various artisans, one of whom seems to have come from Northern Europe. The glass cases contain Medieval and Renaissance examples of goldsmith work, the furnishings of the eighteenth-century Chigi Chapel, the model for Bernini's Saint Jerome (also for the Chigi chapel), the *Golden Rose* given to the Cathedral in 1658 by Pope Alexander VII, and some small wooden sculpture including a dramatic Crucifix by Giovanni Pisano and three polychromed busts of *Saint Crescenzio, Saint Savino* and *Saint Vittore*. The busts were part of a series of seated figures carrying reliquaries executed in 1409 by Francesco di Valdambrino. They are fundamental to an understanding of this sculptor, who was a friend of Ghiberti and a collaborator of Jacopo della Quercia. In other glass cases are wooden models for the twelve Apostles executed by an imitator of Bernini, Giuseppe Mazzuoli, in 1679-'80. The figures were originally placed on the pilasters of the Cathedral and are now in London. The polychromed terracotta of *Saint John the Evangelist Weeping* was once part of a Lamentation group. It is probably the finest work of Giacomo Cozzarelli (1443-1515?), who was inspired by the art of Francesco di Giorgio Martini. A wooden statue of *Saint Savino* is the only one remaining of the four original statues placed at the entrance of the fourteenth-century Cathedral choir. It was made in 1395 by Guido di Giovanni del Tonghio and painted in 1400 by Paolo di Giovanni Fei.

Unknown thirteenth-century artist: Reliquary of the Head of Saint Galgano.

The 'Madonna with big eyes'.

On the top floor of the Museum is a small but select picture gallery. In the center of the first room is a *Madonna* painted on wood, some parts also raised in relief, of the early thirteenth century. Known incorrectly as the "Madonna with big eyes", it is the earliest extant painting of the Sienese school and is additionally famous because of the vow sworn before it on the eve of the battle of Montaperti. On the walls are panels from an altarpiece by Ambrogio Lorenzetti: from the left, *Saint Catherine of Alexandria, Saint Benedict, Saint Francis of Assisi* and *Saint Mary Magdalene.* The central panel, with the Madonna, is missing. Nine small panels, probably from the sacristy cupboards, represent *Articles of the Faith.* These are by Nicola di Naldo da Norcia and were executed in 1412. The *Saint Jerome* is part of an altarpiece from the late period of Giovanni di Paolo (1399-1482). Four coffin decorations by Giovanni Antonio Bazzi called "il Sodoma" (1477-1549) are from the Oratory of San Giovannino beneath the Cathedral. The painting of the *Blessed Agostino Novello,* a masterpiece by Simone Martini was made around 1330 and comes from the Church of Sant'Agostino. Eight large doors (painted on both sides) and two parts of a predella representing *Prophets, Angels* and *Saints,* are from the reliquary cupboard executed in 1411-'12 by Benedetto di Bindo and others for the Cathedral sacristy. On the outside of these doors are thirty-two angels with inscribed scrolls indicating which relic is to be found in the corresponding compartment. On the inside there are eight panels illustrating the *Story of the True Cross.* The work is an excellent work of craftsmanship by a minor painter, perhaps a student of Taddeo di Bartolo, who nonetheless shows a talent for pleasant narrative. The large altarpiece on the center of the wall with the *Madonna* and *Saints Augustine, John the Baptist, Peter and Paul* (1323), is the only signed work by Gregorio di Cecco di Luca, pupil and

Giovanni di Paolo: Apparition of Saint Francis at Arles.

93

adopted son of Taddeo di Bartolo. A small and very brightly colored predella panel of the *Apparition of Saint Francis at Arles* is by Giovanni di Paolo, and another predella panel, this one with the *Crucifixion*, has been attributed to Gregorio di Cecco (early fifteenth century). Finally, we should consider three small panels representing the *Madonna and Child*. The first is a soft and intimate work by Matteo di Giovanni (1425-'95) and comes from the little Church of Percena near Buonconvento. The second is by the very prolific Sienese artist, Sano di Pietro, and the third by a vigorous follower of Duccio called the " Master of Città di Castello ".

The second room of the gallery is called the " Saloncino ", and a plaque and a bust remind us that in this room the great dramatist Vittorio Alfieri acted in his own plays (1777). On the walls, above a series of silk altar frontals embroidered between the fifteenth and eighteenth centuries, is an altarpiece of the *Madonna and Child* with *Saints John the Evangelist, Nicola da Bari, Gregory* and *Jerome.* In the predella are stories from the lives of these saints. The work was executed in 1479 for the Chapel of San Niccolò in the Cathedral. Other works on view are the *Musician Angels* by

Girolamo Magagni, called " Giomo del Sodoma " (1550) and an altarpiece of the *Madonna with Saint Anthony of Padua and Saint Bernardino of Siena* signed Matteo di Giovanni and dated 1460. A *Saint Paul* painted in 1515 by Domenico Beccafumi for the church of the same name (now destroyed), is one of his earliest works and a good example of his splendid sense of color. The background scenes of the conversion and beheading of the apostle contain elements which find their sources in Northern Art; for example, the old woman, the two children and the wind-blown tree. The *Madonna and Child with Saint John* is an early work (1576) by Cristofano Roncalli (" il Pomarancio "); the *Christ before Pilate* and the *Deposition* are by Luca Giordano (1623-1705); and the *Transfiguration*, painted in 1512 by Girolamo Genga, cleary shows the influence of Luca Signorelli. Originally it hung on one of the organs in the Cathedral. The other paintings in this room are of minor importance.

The walls of the next room are covered with velvet tapestries woven with gold (seventeenth century) and a door from the Monastery of the Poor Clares of Campansi with the emblem of the third Franciscan order. The glass cases contain altar

Gregorio di Cecco di Luca: Madonna and Child.

Matteo di Giovanni: Madonna and Child.

frontals, chasubles, and other liturgical vestments of various periods.

A small door at the end of the room leads to the top of the New Cathedral façade. From here one can enjoy the beautiful panorama of Siena with the Cathedral, the Piazza del Campo, the tower " del Mangia ", the austere but grand monastic buildings on the outskirts of the city, and the rolling hills of the surrounding countryside. And from here the enormity of the project for the New Cathedral attempted by the Sienese becomes even more apparent.

Domenico Beccafumi:
Saint Paul.

Essential Bibliography

Ordo Officiorum Ecclesiae Senensis ab Oderico eiusdem Ecclesiae Canonico compositus et nunc primum a.d. Iohanne Crysostomo Trombelli ... editus, Bononise, 1766.

Memorie intorno alle pitture, statue ed altre opere che si ritrovano nel tempio della Cattedrale di Siena lasciate scritte dal Sig. ALFONSO del Sig. POMPILIO LANDI l'anno 1655 - Raccolte dall'ill.mo Sig. CLAUDIO BARGAGLI rettore dell'Opera l'anno 1718. (Mss. in the City Library of Siena, MS.C.II.30).

G. MILANESI, *Documenti per la storia dell'arte senese*, Vol. I-III, Siena, 1854-'56.

S. BORGHESI e L. BANCHI, *Nuovi documenti per la storia dell'arte senese*, Siena, 1898.

V. LUSINI, *Il San Giovanni di Siena*, Firenze, 1901.

R.H. HOBART CUST, *The Pavement Masters of Siena*, London, 1901.

V. LUSINI, *Il Duomo di Siena*, Vol. I, Siena, 1911; Vol. II, Siena, 1939.

P. BACCI, *Jacopo della Quercia*, Siena, 1929.

H. KELLER, *Die Bauplastik des Sieneser Doms*, in « *Jahrbuch der Biblioteca Hertziana* », 1937.

E. CARLI, *Sculture nel Duomo di Siena*, Torino, 1941.

E. CARLI, *Il pulpito di Siena*, Bergamo, 1943.

P. BACCI, *Documenti e commenti per la storia dell'arte*, Firenze, 1944.

E. CARLI, *Il Museo dell'Opera e la Libreria Piccolomini di Siena*, Siena, 1945.

E. CARLI, *Vetrata duccesca*, Firenze, 1946.

E. CARLI, *Una primizia di Jacopo della Quercia*, in « *La Critica d'Arte* », VIII, 1949, pages 17-24.

E. CARLI, *Miniature di Liberale da Verona dai corali del Duomo di Siena*, Milano, 1953.

VARIOUS AUTHORS, *Il restauro della « Maestà » di Duccio*, in « *Bollettino dell'Istituto Centrale del Restauro* », nos. 37-40, 1959.

E. CARLI, *Il Pintoricchio*, Milano, 1960.

E. CARLI, *Michelangelo a Siena*, Roma, 1964.

Z. PEPI, *Il Duomo di Siena*, Siena, 1964.

E. CARLI, *Donatello a Siena*, Roma, 1967.

H.R. MANCUSI UNGARO, *Michelangelo: The Bruges Madonna and the Piccolomini Altar*, New Haven and London, 1971.

M.G. CIARDI DUPRÈ, *I corali del Duomo di Siena*, Milano, 1972.

E. BACCHESCHI e G. CATTANEO, *L'opera completa di Duccio*, Milano, 1972.

J. WHITE, *Measurement, Design and Carpentry in Duccio's Maestà*, in « *The Art Bulletin* », LV, nos. 3-4, 1973.

E. CARLI, *Duccio di Buoninsegna: l'opera autografa* (slide-book), Firenze, 1975.